Becoming Home

Self-Discovery Through the Power of Space

Kendra Jarrell

Raven + Grace
PRESS

Raven and Grace Press

Contents

This book is dedicated to my family, all ya'll! The cousins who are more like siblings, the aunts who have doubled as mothers, and everybody in between. I am truly blessed. You all challenge me, celebrate me, and teach me in ways that force me to never stagnate. Loving you has shaped and stretched me.

A special thank you goes to my husband. This book would not have come together without you. You would. not. let me quit. You held me accountable and believed in me at times when I didn't believe in myself. It takes a special man to honor a strong woman's growth rather than feel threatened by it. Thank you, babe. You make me feel like I have wings.

How to Use This Book

This isn't the kind of book you rush through just to check it off your list. It's the kind of book you live with. One chapter at a time. One small shift at a time. One honest moment at a time.

Every chapter is built like a room in a home, with its own doorway, its own atmosphere, and its own kind of work to be done inside. Some rooms will feel cozy. Others may ask you to pick up a metaphorical hammer and start tearing down old walls. Both are necessary.

A Few Gentle Guideposts:

1. Go at your own pace.

There's no prize for finishing fast. Whether you read this in a weekend or over a season of your life, trust your timing.

2. Make space to reflect.

Each chapter ends with exercises and reflection prompts. These are invitations to explore. You can journal, talk them through, or simply sit with them quietly. There's no wrong way to reflect.

3. Feel your way through it.

Some chapters will stir up emotions you didn't expect. That's part of the process. Give yourself permission to pause, breathe, and come back when you're ready.

4. Use the practices.

Transformation happens when you take what's on the page and live it—whether that's clearing out a closet, setting a boundary, or telling your inner "Cody" to pack up and leave.

5. Make it your own.

Highlight it. Dog-ear it. Scribble in the margins. Talk back to it. This is your story now. By the end, my hope is that this book gives you a blueprint to build and rebuild the spaces that hold your life, both inside and out.

Welcome to *Becoming Home*. Let's get started.

The Decision to Live

There are moments in life so heavy, so relentless, that they blur into a haze of exhaustion and survival. You know, the kind where you don't even realize how much you're carrying until you're crushed beneath the weight of it. I lived in that haze for a long time.

I remember sitting in the doctor's office, and the doctor put me on an antidepressant. I was so confused because my life was "perfect." But for some reason I felt a dark cloud over my head. Some days it felt tough just getting through the day, but I had no idea why. Crying in the kitchen for no apparent reason. I felt so much guilt because I knew so many people had it so much worse than me. What did I have to cry about? I mean, really.

I remember my doctor saying, "You may not be able to know why right now. It may reveal itself later."

And I have to say, she ain't nevah lied.

It came on like a hurricane ending a drought!

My Hurricane

There's one day I remember with painful clarity. I had recently had a violent shift in my circumstances. I was the one people would say, "She's got it toooogethaa!" Then bam!

My body said "Game Over," and I'm on vacation until further notice. And it wasn't just my body. It was my mind, too. I was panicked, anxious, afraid, and terrified of the evenings because I would be alone with my thoughts that terrorized me.

I felt like I was being crushed. Suffocated. All I could see was more of the same. There was no change or relief. Doctors had no answers. Tests gave no insight. But the pain, the weakness, the falling, the darkness, the seizures . . . they Just. Wouldn't. Stop.

There I was. The day everything in me shattered. The day I didn't want to exist anymore.

I was alone in my bedroom, drowning in a silent storm of tears. My body, wrecked from the health crisis I'd been battling since giving birth. My mind, convinced there was no way forward. I prayed, not for help but for a way out. I was asking for permission and a route to end my life. A way to make it all stop. In the only way I thought would be a solution. When I opened my laptop, I wasn't searching for hope. I was searching for an escape plan in the way of how-tos.

But what I found wasn't directions for an exit. It was an answer to how to live. Somehow, instead of methods, I found reasons not to give up. Articles, stories, and voices reminding me that suicide is never the solution. It wasn't what I was looking for, but it was exactly what I needed. Because at that moment, something clicked. If I'm not dying, I need to start living. Not just existing or pushing through, but really truly living.

That decision, one I almost didn't make, changed everything. If you're here, reading this, I have to believe you're standing at your own type of crossroad. Maybe you're exhausted. Maybe you feel lost, stuck, or like life has demanded too much of you for too long. Maybe, like me, you don't even know where the fight in you has gone.

Know this: Your story isn't over. The only way you're guaranteed to lose is if you give up.

But if you choose to keep going? That's where the magic is. That's where you reclaim yourself. That's where you Become Home.

Let's go back to the day I almost didn't make that choice, because everything that came next—the healing, the fight, the transformation—started there.

Chapter 1
Life Happens, But You Decide

The decision to live starts with a quiet spark that asks for more. This chapter begins in that in-between space, where courage hasn't fully caught up, but your feet keep moving anyway. A life-altering moment doesn't just happen. It's the result of a thousand smaller moments, stacking up until one day something cracks. My day of decision was no exception.

The birth of my daughter changed my life forever,but not in the way people imagine when they hear those words. She was unplanned. A surprise. I always wanted to be a mother but never would have had the courage to make that leap through planned parenthood. It just felt too big to take on my choice.

My husband and I were celebrating our eighth wedding anniversary, but that didn't soften the impact of an unexpected shift. I had been sprinting full speed in a completely different direction when motherhood slammed the brakes—hard. It felt like one of those wild mid-air spinouts from The Dukes of Hazzard (yes, I'm dating myself here).

The landing? Not graceful.

Pregnancy knocked me flat. Morning sickness? Try all-day sickness. A nausea so relentless even sounds made it worse. Talking too long? Nausea. Smelling food? Nausea. Too much light?

Nausea. I spent months in a dimly lit room, eyes closed, the only relief coming from soft music. By month four or five, I celebrated being able to watch TV without gagging. That's how bad it was.

Then came the hospital stays with severe dehydration, dizziness, and a weakness that felt like my body had been unplugged from a power strip. But none of that compared to what was happening inside my head.

Before pregnancy, I was driven. Always busy. Always doing. Now, stripped of my ability to outrun my own thoughts, I was left alone with them. They terrified me.

I remember the moment it hit me:standing in the shower, hot water mixing with tears, a realization so sharp it nearly stole my breath.

I was afraid I was going to be a bad mother. I was afraid I was doomed to repeat history. That I would crack under pressure, just like my biological father did when drug abuse took hold of his life. That I would walk away, just like his mother walked out on him, never to return.

I had spent my whole life running from the fear that if given the opportunity at parenthood, I was going to continue a cycle of trauma and pain. But now? Here I was. Nowhere left to run. Having to look my fear dead in the eye. I felt small and scared beside it.

Breaking the Cycle

Here's something I haven't talked about before, not even with some of my closest friends.

When I was two years old, my mother made the hardest,

bravest choice of her life: She left. She walked away from a marriage unraveling under addiction. My biological father was an engineer, a man with a career and a future, but addiction doesn't care about credentials. It steals, consumes, and in his case, spiraled out of control. My earliest memories of him weren't bedtime stories or piggyback rides. They were things disappearing, like valuables and money.

By the time I was five, my mom remarried. When they asked what I wanted to call him, I didn't hesitate. "Daddy," I said. It was never a question in my mind. He became my father in every way that mattered, and years later, we made it official through adoption. Same last name. Same family.

So most people in my life never knew my backstory. If they did, they knew it was a no-fly zone. My dad felt like my dad and still does. All three of us carried pain around the entire situation. It felt too raw to tackle. It was kind of like crisis averted, fire out. Moving on.

For years, I told myself I had escaped my past. That I was one of the "lucky" ones, for lack of a better term. But I never realized that ignoring something doesn't mean it disappears. It just hides, waiting for the right moment to resurface.

Becoming a mother was that moment. All my fears came rushing back.

The Breaking Point

Stress manifests in strange ways.

When my daughter was six months old, my body started shutting down. Dizzy spells. Muscle weakness. Episodes where I couldn't move or speak, where I felt like I was fainting but never lost consciousness. Some days, it happened eleven times. Some days, I couldn't even stand.

I visited doctor after doctor. Received test after test but got no answers.

Then came the day. The day I felt like I had reached the end of my rope. The day I opened my laptop, searching not for help, but for an exit. Yet, somehow, I found the opposite.

Instead of methods, I found reasons.
Instead of an escape, I found hope.
In that moment, something shifted: If I'm not dying, then I need to start living. That moment changed everything.

Rewriting the Story

I made a decision. If the doctors couldn't figure it out, I'd keep going until I did. I hired a personal trainer. I changed my diet. I went to therapy. Hired a coach. Started putting gates on my walls and giving keys to those I trusted. I stopped rejecting help and started accepting it.

Slowly, I found joy again. I learned how to laugh—really laugh. How to stop taking myself so seriously. Our family started going on outings, even if that meant wheelchairs, canes, and walkers.

Here's the truth: We are the writers of our own story. Life doesn't happen to us, but it happens because of us. Yes, circumstances shape us, but they don't have to define us.

Think of it like Mad Libs (is that still a thing?). There's a prewritten story with circumstances we didn't choose. But those blank spaces? That's where the magic happens. That's where we decide what comes next.

So, what if instead of waiting for life to change, we showed it how?

Your Home, Your Power

That brings me to something you might not have considered before, something that changed everything for me: Your environment has power.

We usually think of environment as the outside world—the community you live in, the people around you, or the circumstances you're navigating. Yes, all of that matters, but there's a layer even closer than that.

Your home is a reflection of you, and you are a reflection of your home.

Here's the empowering part: If your space reflects you, then the inverse is true as well. You reflect your space.

Read that again.

If we walk this idea out one more step, we uncover the ultimate life hack: If you want to change yourself, you can change your space. If you want to understand yourself, all you have to do is look around. What I've come to understand is that our homes have a really powerful quality to them because they are equal parts diagnostic and therapeutic. They can reveal us AND remake us.

Let's say it together.

DaaaHHHnnnggg!

Understanding this concept is exactly where we're headed next, as we explore the places you live, the rooms you move through, and the quiet clues your home has been leaving for you all along.

Let's jump in.

Chapter 2

What It Means to "Become Home"

C hange rarely announces itself. It lingers at the edges, quiet and patient, waiting for the moment you're ready to step forward.

Before we dive any deeper, I want us to pause.

Up to this point, you've heard some of my story—the breaking points, the turning points, the moments when I realized something had to change. But if we're going to walk this journey together, we need to be standing on the same foundation.

So let's talk about what this really is. Let's talk about Becoming Home.

Home Isn't Just a Place

When most people hear the word home, they think of a structure: four walls, a roof, maybe a front porch, and a kitchen that smells like something good. More than just a place you live, home is where your life gathers. It's where your energy collects, where your story lingers, where your truth echoes back at you in quiet moments.

Your home is a mirror. It reflects who you are, what you value, and sometimes what you've avoided.

Your home is the most intimate environment you inhabit. It's the space that holds you when no one is watching. It's where your habits live. Where your energy settles. Where your life quietly tells the truth. It's the image minus the filters.

For years, I treated my home as something separate from me, like a locker for my life. A space for my stuff and a pit stop onto the next activity. But I've come to understand that it's far more personal than that. Our home and our internal world are always in conversation. When one shifts, the other responds. It's an unconscious narrative that doesn't have to be crafted. It's intrinsic.

Now I'm warning you, brace yourself, because I'm about to say something really smart. Are we ready? Okay, proceeding…

What feels solid and fixed in your home—your walls, furniture, that extra desk you keep meaning to drop at Goodwill—is made up of constantly moving energy at a microscopic level.

Remember Mr. Einstein and the whole E=mc2 deal. Yea, well that's this. What that means is that your environment isn't static. Your environment is active, responsive, and impacting you, even when you're not paying attention.

You don't just see your home. You experience it.

In your body, thoughts, and energy. It's not only the tangible that's working with you. The things that your senses pick up but that we can't touch are just as powerful:

Lighting → affects mood instantly

Sound → changes stress levels

Air quality → affects energy and clarity

Layout → affects how you move and interact

The space itself is doing work on you. You don't just see your home because you experience it physically and emotionally. The way your space is arranged affects how you move, think, and even what you believe is possible.

Our home and our internal world are always in conversation. When one shifts, the other responds. It's an unconscious narrative that lives within you because the way your home feels influences how you show up. How you show up influences what your home becomes.

It's a loop.

A constant conversation, operating as a feedback system that's always running in the background.

Becoming Home Is a Way of Living

Beyond paint colors or square footage, this book is about what happens when you stop waiting for life to change out there and start cultivating something beautiful right here. Becoming Home is about:

- creating spaces that reflect the person you're becoming

- telling the truth about what's working and what's not

- making small, intentional shifts that ripple into big transformation

- giving yourself permission to take up space in your own story

This is a rhythm, a mindset, a way of living, not a one-time renovation project.

It Happens in the Everyday

You don't have to move across the country to Become Home. You can do it when you clear a single counter. When you hang something on the wall that makes your soul exhale. When you finally toss the thing that's been whispering, "you're stuck here," every time you walk by.

It happens in the quiet choices. The whispered yeses. The decisive nos.

It happens when your external world and your internal self finally start pointing in the same direction.

Your Home Evolves as You Do. Embrace it.

You are not static and neither is your space. Every season of your life writes a new chapter into your walls, your rooms, and your corners. Instead of building a perfect home, the goal is to build a home that grows with you. Some seasons will be about clearing clutter and creating calm. Others will be about daring to dream bigger, changing everything, and starting over. All of them are valid and sacred. All of them are home.

We have to allow space for that growth and to understand: The middle can be messy. It's going to be a little off while it's transitioning. It's like going through the "awkward years" when we have a face only a mother can love.

You know what I'm talking about: snaggletooth, high-water pants, haircut a little too fresh . . . adolescent images that we all try to hide but make our mom smile.

Well, our house has to be allowed to have its own awkward years, too. It's not realistic for us to expect perfection at all times, but especially when we are in a state of becoming.

Release that expectation right now. Write it down. Ball it up. Throw it in the trash because we're going to be done with that right about now. That kind of thinking doesn't serve us. What it does is trap us, making us fearful of moving forward because we don't want to mess up what already works. News flash: It *doesn't* work. That's why you feel the ick.

But don't be scurred! Life and your home come with erasers. When we try something, and we don't like it, guess what? We can change it. We take the failure as feedback and say, "Yikes! Not cute. Won't do that again!"

I remember a time when my mother painted our hallway (I'm gonna get a grown woman whooping for talking about this woman's hallway, but as my grandma used to say, I'm a "tell the truth and shame the devil"). She painted it a deep fuchsia pink and put a black and flowered border in the middle of the wall.

Wow! It was a lot. But you know what? None of us said a word. We knew she was going through something, and we just said, "Okay, so the wall is hot pink." It's just paint, and that hot pink hallway ended up a beautiful creamy white.

Messy middles. The awkward years. They have erasers. Let's give ourselves the permission and space to iterate. Remember, this is *your* life and *your* house, and in the words of OutKast, "That's my house, I disconnect the cable and turn the lights out…"

Why This Matters

If you only take one thing from this chapter, let it be this: The way we shape our spaces shapes us back. Not just emotionally or aesthetically, but in our brains and bodies. Whether we realize it or not.

When we become intentional about the homes we build, both physically and emotionally, we stop living as bystanders in our own lives. We stop waiting for something external to unlock us. We become the key.

What's Next

The rest of this book will walk you through real stories, practical steps, and soul-level shifts. This chapter is your compass.

When things get messy—and they will—come back here. When you're tired, when you doubt, when you forget why this matters, return to this anchor.

Becoming Home isn't about where you live. It's about who you're becoming.

Chapter 3
Your Home Reflects All of You

G rowth starts in the quiet space where fear tries to whisper its lies, and courage chooses to speak louder.

A Breath and a Beginning

Take a breath.
No, really—in and out.

We've just cracked open some soul-level stuff, and now it's time to shift gears. Not to skip past the hard parts, but to pivot from introspection to action.

Here's the quiet truth I've learned: When your environment starts to change, you do, too.

It's not magic, but momentum. We tend to overcomplicate the big life shifts. We want a neon sign from the universe saying, "Now is the time!" But more often than not, the sign looks suspiciously like your kitchen table. Or that pile of stuff in the corner. Or a room that doesn't quite feel like you anymore.

Here's the cheat code: Impact the outer, and you'll impact the inner.

That's where we begin.

Defining the Outer and the Inner

Let's keep this simple:

- The inner is everything that lives in your head and heart: dreams, fears, limiting beliefs, that running commentary that doesn't know when to hush.

- The outer is everything you can touch: your home, your desk, your bedroom, that laundry pile staring you down right now.

The outer is the lever. It's the thing we can actually do something about when the inner feels slippery and stuck. Sometimes, the fastest way to get unstuck emotionally is to pick up a sock.

What "Home" Really Means

Whenever I record my podcast, I end every conversation with one question: "What does home mean to you?"

The answers are as varied as fingerprints.

- A 3-year-old might say, "It's where I live."

- A 10-year-old might say, "It's a place and a feeling."

- A homesick college student will probably whisper, "Home is what you make it."

Home shape-shifts. It grows with us. It stretches, contracts, and sometimes sags in the middle like an old couch that's seen some things. That's why this book is about learning how to come back to yourself, again and again, through the spaces you inhabit.

The Game Be Gamein'

Life is a game. A messy, unpredictable, sometimes hilarious basketball game. The best moments happen, not in the blowout wins, but in the back-and-forth, the chaos, and the clutch moves that shouldn't have worked but did.

The game be gamein', just like life be lifein'. The best players don't wait for a clean shot. They create one. That's what I want for you: to learn how to create your own openings.

Happiness Is an Inside Job

When I was a tween, sobbing over some middle-school drama that felt like the end of the world, my mom would hit me with two truths:

1. Don't sweat the small stuff.

2. Happiness is an inside job.

She didn't say it sweetly, either—it was more of a "wipe your face and get it together" vibe. She was teaching me that outside chaos doesn't get to own my peace. A lesson that, inconveniently, turned out to be right.

The Lightbulb Moment

Years later, there I was, a grown woman and business owner, sitting in my car furious. My business was stuck. Stalled out. Like a car at a green light with no gas when it hit me—clean, quiet, undeniable.

My house looked exactly like my business. For the first time, I didn't just feel frustrated. I saw a pattern. The structure was there. The vision was there. But the finishing touches?

Still in boxes. Curtains still packaged. Wallpaper still rolled. Organizational bins collecting dust.

My home mirrored my life. I'd built the thing, but I hadn't fully moved into it. What surprised me most wasn't the realization itself. It was how it came to me. Not in a strategy meeting or a coaching session, but in the pause.

A quiet moment where I finally stopped powering through and let myself feel how uncomfortable I was. I didn't talk myself out of it. I didn't distract myself from it. I let the frustration get loud enough to teach me something. Once I did, the rest followed naturally.

I could trace the feeling back to its source. I could see where my inner resistance was living, not just in my thoughts but in my space. For the first time, I knew exactly where to start. I didn't need to blow everything up or a new five-year plan. I needed to change what I could see and trust that the shift would ripple inward.

That moment became the way out.

I didn't call it anything then. I was just trying to breathe again, but looking back, I can see it clearly now.

That pause. . .That awareness . . . That decision to modify what was right in front of me. That was the moment I understood that our homes are not passive backdrops. They are mirrors.

That was the beginning of what I now call the Becoming Home Method™.

Before you start getting bass in your voice, yelling at the book . . . Don't worry, boo. I got you. I lay out the full Becoming Home Method in the appendix. No secrets. All the tea. You'll know exactly how to use it.

Doing It Scared

So I did the thing. Not because I felt brave—I was just tired of feeling stuck, like I should be further than I was.

Like I had all the advantages but none of the results. Like I was playing musical chairs with just one chair and one player, but still somehow the music never stopped. I couldn't see where it was coming from or when it would end. All I knew was I was exhausted from circling the chair, waiting for permission to sit down.

I sorted. Donated. Installed. Adjusted. Somewhere between the half-opened boxes and the new curtain rods, I realized that I'd been afraid. Afraid of letting go of old versions of me and to really take up space. Then, just like that, something cracked open.

I stopped apologizing for my style. I went bold. Dramatic. Unapologetically me. Dark blue wallpaper, Matisse abstract art, repurposing rooms and layouts to fit our life. Forget the dining room—I want a conversation lounge instead. Third bedroom? How about a moody library. Gray office walls? Let there be pale coral and greenery!

And, yes, it was messy, so is becoming.

The Mirror Effect

As my house shifted, so did my business. I cut the clutter, both the literal and metaphorical kind. I dropped services that drained me. Hired help where I needed it. Aligned my work with what actually lit me up. This wasn't a carefully architected "transformation journey." It was just me . . . picking up junk.

Pick up the junk. Sweep the floor. Do the dishes. That's all the brilliance you need to get started.

The Power Pause: Small Shifts, Big Impact

I call these moments The Power Pause, because when we stop with intention, the pause itself becomes powerful. Pick one or all. Pick the one that makes you roll your eyes because it's probably the one that'll work.

Option 1: Room-by-Room Reflection

Record a casual video walkthrough of your home. Say out loud how each room makes you feel. Watch it back (yes, cringe is part of the process). Notice patterns.

Option 2: Photo Review

Take a photo of each room. Rate it 1–5 on comfort, inspiration, and function. Ask yourself why. Notice the theme your space is whispering back to you.

Finding the Why

There's always a why. Why the pile stays. Why the curtain rod is still in the box. Why the idea never quite gets off the ground. If we don't stop and name the why, we keep looping.

Like the road trip where my mom and I missed our turn and ended up circling the same McDonald's over and over. We kept trying to get back on track, and it really seemed like we were taking a different route each time we tried to recover. But inevitably we kept passing the saaame McDonald's. It felt like the road trip version of the movie *Groundhog Day*. No exaggeration! The only way we got out was stopping the car, calling my then boyfriend (now husband), and getting him to pull out his map to trace our steps and direct us out of the McDonald's vortex. We had to name the why. There was a reason we weren't making progress and kept finding ourselves in the same loop.

Your McDonald's might be a room, habit, or belief. But trust me, it's there. There is always a "why" to being stuck, to thinking we're doing things differently but ending up with the same result.

Start Back at One

Here's what we know: Change is hard. We can make it simpler, and shifting your outer world can unstick your inner one. So start where you are. Light a candle. Clear a surface. Move one thing.

In the words of Brian McKnight, "If ever I believe my work is done, I'll start back at one." This is about coming home to yourself.

Next up: the beliefs that keep us boxed in. Time to break some stuff!

Chapter 4
Shattering Limiting Beliefs

Becoming is about choosing to keep moving in an intentional direction agnostic of the rate of speed or length of time.

The Stretch Before the Shift

Here's the thing about transformation—it starts with an itch. That quiet irritating awareness that something isn't quite right anymore. We can change the curtains, light a candle, and rearrange the furniture, but deep down, we know that's not the whole story. Real change asks us to stretch just far enough to feel it.

It's like when your husband puts the cereal on the top shelf after you specifically told him not to.

Oh, you could grab a stool, but you don't. It's not about cereal anymore, it's the principle. So you reach. You stretch, and you feel ridiculous. The kind of ridiculous where you hope no one's behind you with their phone out, because if this goes south, you're one viral video away from cereal-aisle fame.

But even with the threat of public humiliation, something in you says, "I have to do this."

It's the yellow-light moment.

No reverse. No reroute.
You're going to have to floor it.

You know the feeling. When you can taste what's possible, and you realize you'll never feel complete until you see it through. That's transformation, an awkward, uncomfortable, a reach with risk that demands something deeper than décor.

The Sneakiest Blockers: Limiting Beliefs

In the coaching world, we call this resistance limiting beliefs. Think of them as your brain's default safety protocols. Most of us inherit them without even realizing it, from parents, culture, or the communities we grew up in.

The tricky part? They're sneaky. They don't wave their hands in the air and say, "Hey, I'm a limiting belief!" They dress themselves up as virtue, as caution, as practicality, as something meant to keep us safe.

It's like that hidden pop-up blocker on your computer that you don't even know is running until it suddenly keeps you from getting where you want to go.

Limiting beliefs are loyal little guards. They don't show themselves until you try to step outside the fence they've built. That's exactly why changing your environment can feel so uncomfortable because it sets off the alarm.

The Back-Door Approach

One reason the Becoming Home Method works is because we don't storm the front gate. We slip in through the back door. We change the external first, and by the time those limiting beliefs realize what happened, they've got no fight left.

How to Hack the System:
Change the external to overwrite limiting beliefs.

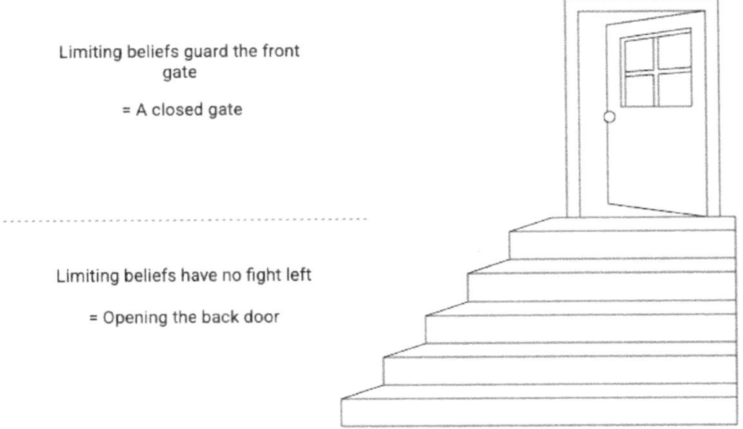

That doesn't mean you have to name every limiting belief today. You don't have to air out your entire emotional filing cabinet.

What you can do is turn up the volume of your thoughts. Slow down enough to actually hear the quiet fears that run in the background of your daily decisions. If you can't hear them, you can't challenge them.

The Move That Changed Everything

The first time I really noticed my limiting beliefs was when we decided to move out of our starter home.

That house held a lifetime of memories. It was family central—drop-offs, cousins running through the yard, the long goodbyes in the driveway when family heads back home, and my grandma cooking while simultaneously bossing everyone around. It was the heartbeat of my family.

But underneath all those warm memories was something heavy. I'd always wanted to move across town, and that desire terrified me.

Why?

No one with brown skin lived there. Moving felt like turning my back on everything that made me. Deep down, I believed wanting more meant I was saying, "I'm too good for you."

So for years, I stayed. Mind you these were stories, narratives I told myself were true. They were rooted in my perception, but not in a reflective reality, because what I thought I hadn't seen, I really had.

The truth was before my parents, there was no one with brown skin who lived in our current neighborhood either. You still could count them on two hands. So this was MY OWN limiting belief I was telling myself as an excuse, because it kept me safe from what felt like a stretch.

Doing It Anyway

Then I became a mother. Our family had grown, our house hadn't, and it was time to face the thing I'd been avoiding.

I didn't suddenly feel brave. Instead, I had to use logic to give myself courage. The logic? We'd renovated it. We'd outgrown the space. It was time.

I didn't fully understand it then, but I was allowing my limiting beliefs to auto-steer my life. That pattern had kept me "safe" in a version of life that no longer fit. I believed I had to stay where I'd always been until I decided not to.

That move changed everything. It required me to shatter a belief that had quietly dictated my choices for years.

You see it wasn't just about that house but what the house represented. It was a home my parents had chosen, not me. I had already tried to work with it and make it my own. But it wasn't enough. I also didn't want to draw attention to myself. If I sold the family home, it would be a conversation point. Even in passing, I didn't want to be a topic of conversation.

My life was in the same situation. I chose a career that was accessible, but wasn't something I truly enjoyed. I had tried doing career adjacent things with consulting, but it still wasn't quite right. I just wanted to be as invisible as possible, because if someone saw me they might have an opinion about me, and it might be that they didn't like me.

Do you see the mirror reflection? And why that move was the catalyst of so much? I can tell you a similar home-translates-to-life story in Every. Single. Home. Coincidence? I think not. But this kind of shift is never easy.

Why It Feels So Heavy

When we challenge a limiting belief, we're not just making a practical change. We're shaking the foundation of how we've felt safe. On the other side of that discomfort is alignment. You build a bridge to a life that looks and feels more like your truest self.

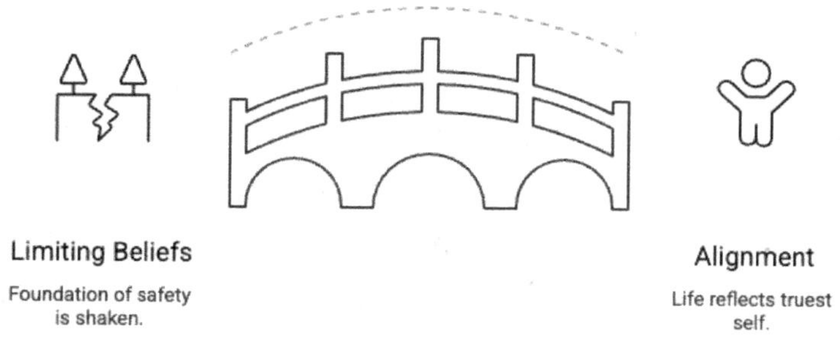

Start Reaching

Limiting beliefs are rarely loud. They whisper. They blend in. But the moment you stretch—when you decide to go for what's just out of reach—they show themselves. That's your cue. That's where the work begins.

You don't have to be fearless. You just have to reach anyway.

The Power Pause: Finding the Fence Posts

Pick the one that calls you—or the one that makes you roll your eyes, because that's usually the one doing the heavy lifting.

Option 1. Limiting Belief Journal

Write down one limiting belief you've held about your home or your life.
Examples:
   "I don't belong in that neighborhood."
   "I can't afford something better."
   "People like me don't live like that."

Then, list three reasons it isn't true or reframe it into a statement of power.
Example: "I am deserving of a space that makes me feel safe and inspired."

Option 2. Self-Talk Audit

Throughout the day, pay attention to your inner dialogue.

Every time you catch yourself thinking, "I can't," "That's not for me," or "I shouldn't," write it down.

At the day's end, pick one belief to actively challenge over the next week.

What Lies Ahead

Stretching isn't comfortable. But comfort was never the goal. Alignment is.

Once you name what's been holding you back, the next step is to rebuild from the inside out.

Next up: What happens when we choose to rebuild the home within.

Chapter 5
Rebuilding the Home Within

The stories we tell ourselves can keep us safe or keep us stuck. But the moment we name them, we give ourselves permission to rewrite them.

The Wobbly First Steps

Okay, so here we are. We've stretched. We've done the thing that felt uncomfortable.

Now what?

We might feel like a toddler who just took their first steps, thrilled, wobbly, and one sneeze away from face-planting into the carpet. That moment right after courage is one of the most vulnerable places to be. It's when the adrenaline wears off and reality starts whispering, *"Oh snap! What have I done?"*

That's exactly how I felt after we built our custom home. I'd sprinted through the excitement, then BAM, slammed the brakes. I didn't have a map or a guide. I just had that wide-eyed feeling of "now what?"

Courage Is the Door, Not the Destination

Courage opens the door, but it's not the house itself.

What gets us through the next part is structure. A plan. A way to steady ourselves when everything feels new and unfamiliar.

Here's something most people don't realize: Nothing in your life is neutral. In physics, there's a principle that says for every action, there is a reaction. That doesn't just apply to objects. It applies to your life too.

- The way you think → shapes what you do

- What you do → creates patterns

- Those patterns → create the life you're living

From Thought to Reality

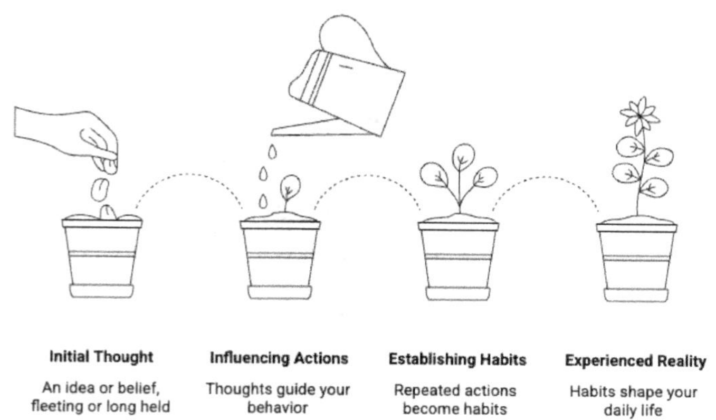

And your home?

That's one of the clearest places those patterns show up.

Your home isn't random. Your routines? Not random. The way you feel when you walk into your space? Not random.

It's all a series of reactions to actions you've taken, consciously or unconsciously, that have brought you to this space, right here, right now.

Think about it in terms of your literal house. How would you feel if the builder showed up and said, "Yep I got a general idea of what you want. We don't need blueprints. You can save some money on that. I'll make sure to tell all the contractors what you asked for."

You'd tell the joker to kick rocks. So why do we do the equivalent to ourselves by approaching life with an "I hope it works out" attitude? No ma'am. When we're structured for nothing, that's exactly what we get.

From Courage to Structure

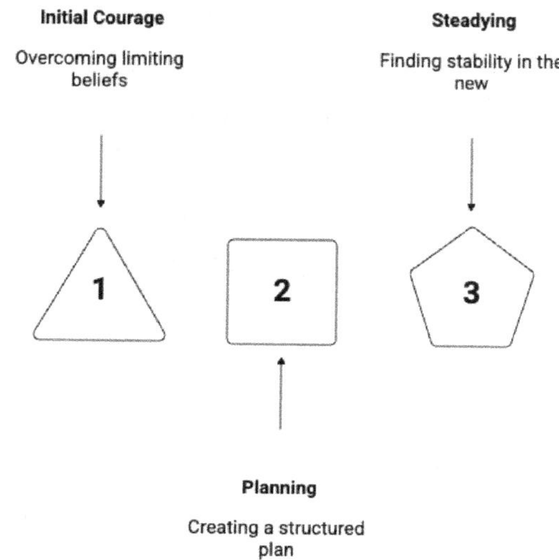

Sounds great right? Before we can plan anything, we have to allow ourselves the permission to do so. And what I've come to see in my own life and the lives of those I've coached, is that often the reason we haven't planned for our success, isn't because of laziness or lack of motivation. It's because we have a blocker there. Those blocks are our limiting beliefs. When I look back at that dark season of my life, I can see it clearly now. The moment I challenged my limiting beliefs it gave me the bravery to plan, because in order to plan you have to be able to dream.

Dreaming requires that we believe something is possible and probable. We can't do that without our own buy in.

Standing up to those limiting beliefs was the spark. What came next was the flame, and I didn't even know it was happening.

The Light Switch Moment

One ordinary morning, something shifted. It was after that first big move into that new neighborhood. It felt like someone had flipped a switch inside me and the lights came back on. I started claiming my mornings. Planning trips. Dreaming bigger. Slowly, doing things I had never seen modeled before.

That's where my entrepreneurial journey truly began. Not at a fancy event or with some grand epiphany, but in the quiet aftermath of a decision I almost didn't make. Had I not taken that leap, I wouldn't have discovered the version of me waiting on the other side of fear.

Looking back now, I can see something deeper was happening. I wasn't just "changing my mindset." I was interrupting a pattern.

Our brain doesn't just respond to what you decide; it responds to what you repeat. Every thought you revisit, every behavior you practice, every environment you sit in, your brain is wiring around it. Which means the life you're experiencing isn't just something that happened to you. It's something that has been built—piece by piece—through repetition.

Once you see that, something shifts because if it was built, it can be rebuilt.

Hope and Faith, Not Perfect Formulas

Here's the real talk: Transformation isn't tidy. It doesn't follow a clean timeline or come with step-by-step IKEA instructions.

If you need proof, think about the last time you painted a room. When you're slap in the middle, the place and you are a legit disaster zone. I mean, call FEMA, 'cause this is the real deal! You've lived it. Transformation. Isn't. Tidy.

This next part? It's about faith. Faith that, just like a house, you can be remodeled. That you can tear down walls, rebuild, and make space for something new.

Where there's life, there's hope. Where there's hope, there's power to choose. Sometimes you only recognize transformation in the rear-view mirror, when you catch a glimpse of a braver version of yourself.

Transformation isn't tidy, but it is consistent. Even when it feels chaotic, there's patterns underneath it.

Think about it like this: If you avoid something long enough, it doesn't disappear. It compounds.

Avoidance turns into anxiety. Clutter turns into overwhelm. Indecision turns into stagnation.

Those aren't random emotions. They're reactions.

Your life is always responding to you. The question is: Do you like what it's saying back?

The Blueprint Within

Think of your inner world like a home. Sometimes we live in the same floor plan for years because it's familiar, even when it no longer fits.

But here's the deeper truth: Your life is a system, and your home is one of the clearest outputs of that system. It reflects what you prioritize, what you delay, what you tolerate, and even what you invest in.

When something feels "off," the goal isn't to judge it. It's to read it. When we read it, no drama is required. We don't have to obsess and get emotional about what it's telling us. Read it as historical facts translated into an environment. It doesn't define you.

The line I live by is "It's not failure, it's feedback." That applies to our houses too. Our home is simply communicating the person we are or used to be. Yes, sometimes we live in the same floor plan for years because it's familiar, even when it no longer fits. That doesn't mean we can't renovate. It doesn't mean we can't knock down a wall that's been blocking the light or build something sturdier beneath us.

Change doesn't just happen in the rooms around us. It happens in the spaces within us.

Remodeling Yourself on Purpose

Pause and hear me on this…You are not a static structure. You are a living, breathing system. Which means change doesn't happen in one big moment. It happens through small inputs, repeated over time.

> 1 decision + 1 shift + 1 new pattern = Momentum.

Momentum makes you unstoppable.

That's how momentum builds. Momentum is powerful because once something is in motion, it tends to stay in motion. Even if you don't like the direction. That's why people feel stuck. Not because nothing is happening, but something is happening over and over again. (Ya'll remember Newton's Third Law of Motion from physics class? Where here it is in living color).

I remember P.E. class in second grade when we were learning T-Ball. I was at bat, swung, and hit who knows what. Instead of the ball flying forward, it dropped straight down to the ground. Then one of the boys yelled, "My dead grandma could hit better than that!"

I was equal parts embarrassed and angry. But the fact remained that once that ball was dropping to the ground, it was going to continue to drop to the ground. I couldn't change that because I wanted it to fly into the outfield and shut that kid's pie hole. The law is law; once something is in motion it continues in motion. Period.

When we understand the power of momentum in our space, it no longer has to take us prisoner. We can use it intentionally to make powerful, vision centered shifts to create deep lifestyle design.

It's you as the vision board. You're a living, breathing home, capable of being reimagined, remodeled, and rebuilt.

So grab your metaphorical blueprint. Tear down what no longer fits. Build what does. When you rebuild the home within, everything around you begins to shift, too. This is where the story becomes yours.

Your Life Is Responding to You

I remember the moment I realized that my life wasn't happening to me. It was responding to me. Every decision I made, every delay, and "I'll get to it later"…

It was all creating something. And once I saw that, I couldn't unsee it because it meant I had more power than I thought. Not to control everything but to influence what came next. That meant, instead of saying, "I'll clean out my closet when I have time." I needed to get up and get to work.

We Build in the Everyday

Remember that you are already building. Every day. With your thoughts, your actions, and your patterns. The only question is: Are you building on purpose?

The Power Pause: A Simple Reset Exercise

Instead of jumping straight into big changes, let's start with awareness. Think of this as observing your life like a system. Small inputs create different outputs.

Choose one area:
- your home

- your schedule

- your energy

- your mindset

No blame. Just clarity.

Now ask yourself:
- What am I experiencing right now?

- What does it feel like?

- Then go one layer deeper:

- What patterns might have created this?

Then ask: What is one small shift I could make that would create a different outcome?

Chapter 6
When "I Can't" Becomes "I Won't"

Change is the quiet shift inside your own four walls that reminds you how powerful you already are.

The Power Hiding in Plain Sight

At some point in life, we all bump up against the thing we tell ourselves we can't do. Rather than judgment, this chapter is about truth—the kind that cracks open doors you thought were locked.

Here's the quiet shift most people never name out loud: "I can't" isn't always the end of the story. Sometimes, it's just a cover for "I won't."

That moment where you say, "I can't" isn't just a thought.

It's a signal, and your life responds to it. The thoughts you repeat become the actions you take. The actions you take become the patterns you live in. Those patterns shape the results you see.

So when you say "I can't," your life listens. And it responds accordingly.

My Pet Peeve with "I Can't"

You know how you can tell you really know someone when you know not just what they love, but what drives them nuts? Here's one of mine: I hate when people say, "I can't."

I've heard it all:

"I can't buy a house."

"I can't live in that neighborhood."

"I can't qualify for a loan."

"I can't afford an agent."

So here I go, "Ms. Fix-It". I took those words at face value. I'm a puzzle-solver by nature, so I'd charge in like a woman on a mission. I'd run the numbers, find solutions, and blow their minds with how possible it actually was.

Then . . . they'd walk away. Every. Single. Time.

I thought I was solving the problem. The only issue was I was solving the wrong problem. I thought people needed more information, better options, stronger strategies. But that wasn't it.

They didn't have a logistics problem when they were telling me, "I can't…". They had a pattern problem because when someone believes "I can't," their brain starts filtering reality to prove it.

It looks for confirmation and ignores possibility. It shuts down options before they're even explored. Even when a solution is right in front of them, they can't see it because their lens won't let it in.

What "I Can't" Really Means

It took me a while to realize what was actually happening. When someone said, "I can't," what they often meant was "I won't."

"I can't" sounds like there's no choice. It hands your power to something outside yourself. "I won't" puts the power back in your hands. It's a statement of agency.

Agency is your ability to make choices and own them. And here's where this gets real: Your choices don't just stay in your head. They show up in your environment.

You delay organizing → your space reflects indecision
You avoid decisions → your environment feels unfinished
You overextend → your home feels chaotic

Your home is responding to you, not judging or punishing you. Responding. When we take agency of our environment we acknowledge we have a voice in what happens next. You take power of attorney in your own life.

When we say, "I can't," we surrender that voice. We step out of the driver's seat and into the backseat, just along for the ride, like you're a toddler instead of a grown woman.
But when we say, "I won't," we put ourselves in the driver's seat… we take back the wheel and a controlling interest. Even if the road is hard, at least now we're the ones steering.

"I can't" leaves us stuck with no next step. "I won't" invites us to ask the real question: Why not? What's under the surface: fear, shame, a belief we inherited?

Here's the truth that stings a little but frees a lot. We say "I can't" because it feels safer. If it's not up to us, we can't fail or disappoint ourselves. We get to stay wrapped in what we know. But safety and power don't always live in the same house.

Bridging the Gap: Belief Is the Key

Once we tell ourselves the truth, something powerful happens. We stop being stuck in "I can't" and start living in "I choose."

When you say, "I can't"… you reinforce limitation. When you repeat, "I choose"… you build momentum.

When people believe change is possible—even if nothing around them has changed yet—they begin to move.

This is exactly what I saw in my own life after we made our first big move. Remember how I talked about challenging my limiting belief of stepping out of the "norm"? Something surprising happened afterward.

My courage created a ripple effect. People who had never voiced their dreams started sharing them with me, quietly at first, like they were testing if hope was allowed. They whispered dreams of moving, building, and starting fresh. They didn't need me to fix anything. They just needed to see someone like them go first.

When There's No Example

Here's the truth: it's not always realistic to wait for someone else to go first. Sometimes, there's no validation, no cheerleading squad, no blueprint.

Sometimes, you're the one who has to take the first step and let others follow—or not. And if no one joins your party? That's fine.

As India Arie said, "I'm having a private party. Ain't nobody here but me, my angels, and my guitar."

You have to believe in your own change. Even if it's quiet. Even if no one else sees it yet.

The Power of Perspective

If you look at "I can't," as a lens on how we experience life, we see that our brain is constantly predicting what's going to happen next based on what it already believes.

If your belief is "I can't," your brain prepares you for that limitation. But! if your belief shifts to "I choose," your brain starts preparing you for possibility.

The situation hasn't changed, but your response has. And as Gomer Pyle used to say, "Shazahm!" because that's where everything begins to shift.

For me, that inner shift—the thing that made me fight when things got hard—came with motherhood. It was about the lens I learned to see the world through after becoming a mother. That no-quit, won't-stop grit comes from loving someone so deeply you'd fight to the death to protect them.

It's the kind of resolve that says there is no option but forward. That was the powerful lens hiding underneath the monkey junk of my mental baggage, when I thought I might be doomed to repeat history.

"I can't" is more than words. It's the lens you're looking through when you say it. When we say, "I can't," we look through the lens of "I quit." When we quit, there's nowhere to go. How can you get a raise on a job you already quit? It's already done. Nowhere to go but down. When has someone ever said, "I can't," then come up with a solution to a problem? Let me help you out. . .Nevaahhh.

Think about going to the eye doctor. You're asked to read line two, and you squint and fumble through it. Then they swing that big contraption in front of you and make tiny adjustments.

The chart hasn't changed. But your lens has. When we change the lens and view life through gratitude, possibility, and agency, everything sharpens. "I can't" starts to dissolve.

Stop waiting for the world to hand you permission. You're already creating results, whether you realize it or not. Every thought and action, for better or worse. It's all producing something.

Now the question is: Is it producing what you want?

Owning the Choice

Here's the connection:

- "I can't" keeps us stuck behind a foggy lens, convinced the world is unchangeable.

- "I won't" clears the lens and puts the power back in our hands.

When we shift how we speak to ourselves, we start to see the world differently. When we see differently, we act differently.

You don't need to wait for someone to hand you permission. You can hand it to yourself. You can keep saying "I can't" and wait for the world to change. Or you can say "I won't" and start changing the world you live in.

The difference isn't just language. It's the power of intentional programming to curate the result you want. The life you give yourself permission to own. It's the moment your life stops waiting for someone else to steer.

The difference isn't just language but power. It's permission. It's the moment your life stops waiting for someone else to steer.

You gotta show up if you want the glow up. Ya heard?

The Power Pause: Turning "I Can't" Into "I Won't"

These exercises invite you to step back into your power, one sentence and one choice at a time.

Option 1: Mindset Check-In

1. Write down five things you've been telling yourself you can't do.

2. Reframe each as "I won't" and ask yourself why.

3. For each one, set a single small action that moves you one step closer to "I can."

Option 2: Mindset Challenge

1. For the next week, catch yourself every time you say "I can't" out loud or in your thoughts.

2. Pause. Reframe it to "I choose not to."

3. Keep a daily log. Watch how this one small shift changes how you feel and what you do.

The Turning Point

This is the moment you stop waiting for the world to hand you permission. "I can't" was a cage. "I won't" is the key.

Once you've got the key, you can unlock a space that works for you, not against you. This is where language becomes movement. Where mindset meets momentum. Next, we're turning that power into action—one drawer, one corner, one room at a time.

Chapter 7

Your Home Is a Platform for Growth

Action doesn't have to be bold or loud. Sometimes, it's the quiet, shaky step no one sees, but the one that changes everything.

Turning the Lens Toward You

Up until now, I've shared a lot of my story: the fears, the shifts, the moves, the lightbulb moments.

But this next part? This is where the story becomes yours.

While moving homes was a major part of my personal journey, the real transformation was about what those spaces represented. Change doesn't always require a moving truck. You don't need a new address to create a new atmosphere. You can begin right where you are.

There's a concept in psychology you may have heard of, Maslow's Hierarchy of Needs. At its core, it says before we can grow into who we're meant to be, our basic needs have to be met first. Think of it like a pyramid.

- At the bottom: You need rest. Safety. Stability.

- In the middle: You need connection. Belonging. Support.

- At the top: You reach for purpose. Growth. Becoming.

Your home plays a role in every single level of that pyramid.

Your Space, Your Power

There's a direct line between the space we occupy and the space between our ears, and science backs that up. Your environment is constantly influencing how you feel, how you think, and what you believe is possible.

If your space feels chaotic, your brain has to work harder just to feel calm.

If your environment feels safe and supportive, your mind has room to expand.

Our homes either support our growth or slow it down. There's no neutral ground here. Your environment is more than a backdrop—it's a platform. It holds you, mirrors you, and shapes how you move through your days.

The best part? It's actionable today. You can transform your environment in three simple, deeply powerful ways:

- organizing

- decorating and design

Tackle them in that order:

1. Cleaning and decluttering

2. Organizing

3. Decorating and design

Remember I said, "Your home plays a role in every single level of that (Maslow's) pyramid." Well, here it is in application.

At the bottom: Cleaning and decluttering answer our physiological needs, creating safety and a restful   atmosphere.

In the middle: Organizing creates a connection of purpose. Items that belong together are now properly grouped and can support the true function of the space.

At the top: We have decorating and design. This is where the real fun begins! Once you have the proper foundation of your cleaning and decluttering you can create growth. And Becoming Home™ in its most transformative form, lifestyle design.

I want to give you a simple way to think about this. I call it The Home Transformation Pyramid™.

Can you see visually how transforming your space—and your life—doesn't happen all at once? It happens in layers, from the ground up.

When we treat our homes with respect, including the things and the people inside it, we remind ourselves that we are worthy of respect, too. When we curate our spaces to reflect who we are becoming, they stop holding us back and start lifting us up.

Why Your Environment Matters More Than You Think

Let's look at your home as a place where your nervous system resets. It's where your habits are formed and where your identity is reinforced.

So if your space is constantly sending signals like:

- unfinished

- overwhelming

- temporary

- not quite right

Your brain starts to believe that about your life, too. But when your space says:

- intentional

- calm

- clear

- aligned

You start showing up differently. That's the shift.

The "Why Didn't We Do This Sooner?" Moment

Have you ever watched one of those design shows where a team swoops in, refreshes a home, and the owners are left in tears saying, "Why didn't we do this a long time ago?"

That moment always hits me. Sometimes our first instinct when something feels broken is to run. To escape. But often, the most powerful transformation comes from staying.

- Putting in the sweat equity.

- Finding and fixing what's broken.

- Cleaning what's dirty.

- Tossing what no longer serves you.

- Painting the walls and saying, "This space deserves care, because I do, too."

That moment always hits because it reveals something simple but powerful. The transformation wasn't out of reach. It was just unaddressed. Because you don't need a completely different life to feel better. Sometimes you just need to change what your life is responding to.

The Weight of Staying

Staying can feel harder than packing a box. Staying asks you to face the dust you've ignored. It asks you to take ownership. It forces you to see yourself clearly in the mirror of your environment.

That's where the power lives. Not in running away from the discomfort, but in standing in it and saying, "I can build something new right here."

Staying asks you to face what's been quietly building over time; because nothing in your home just appears overnight.

It's all built through small decisions.
What you kept.
What you delayed.
What you ignored.
What you invested in.
Your home is the result of those patterns, and that's actually good news.

The Internal Renovation

Here's the quiet truth tucked inside this action: When we choose to invest in our current space, we're also investing in ourselves. We learn not to run at the first sign of discomfort. We learn to stand, face the moment, and say, "I'm worth this effort."

Because you are.

This is about your heart, your energy, your future. No excuses. Just action.

You can do hard things.

Here's the quiet truth tucked inside this action: When you invest in your space, you also rewire your experience. You're teaching your brain:

- This matters.

- I matter.

- This is worth my effort.

And over time, those small signals build something bigger. Think confidence and clarity. Think momentum in the direction you actually want to go!

Understanding What Matters in the Right Now

Don't twist up what I'm telling you here. Just like I shared from my own path, sometimes it's time to schedule the moving truck, sis. What I've learned—both in my life and in working with others—is that our home has to support where we are in life and what's taking priority.

As we journey through life, our priorities don't stay the same. When your priorities shift, your environment has to shift with them. I call this the Pyramid of Priority. At different stages of life, different things rise to the top.

Sometimes you're focused on survival, stability, affordability, just getting through.

Like when you have a newborn on your hands and it's a real win if you're showered and your hair made it into a messy bun. Ain't nobody thinking about flower arrangements or paint swatches. Not the priority!

Sometimes it's about connection, family, routine, building a life that feels grounded.

Like when that kid gets a little older and you really want them to have grandparents nearby and a good school district. Ain't nobody worrying about walkable nightlife. We got big-girl problems and bills. Get this dag condo sold!

And sometimes, you reach for something more, alignment, purpose, becoming who you know you're meant to be.

Like when that kid is about to leave the nest and we start dreaming of building a custom home in the place we've always secretly dreamed of living. Our priority is shifting...

None of these are wrong. They're seasons. But here's the key: Your home has to match the season you're in. That's where The Pyramid of Priority helps us. It makes sense of those times when we no longer feel nurtured by our environment and feel the need for a shift.

The Pyramid of Priority

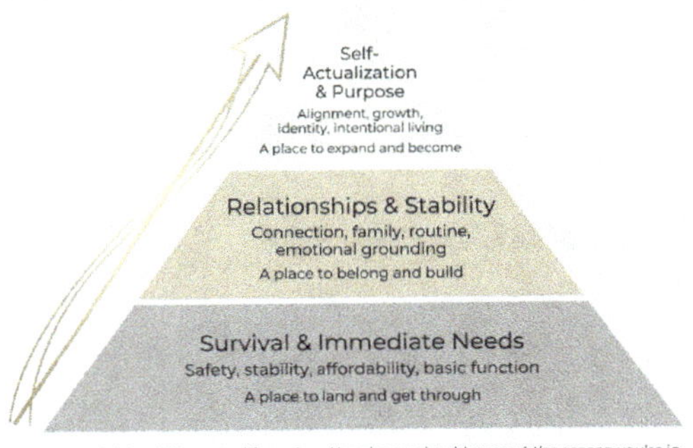

Just because something once fit your life, doesn't mean it's meant to fit forever. Growth doesn't mean you chose wrong before. It means your life is asking for something new now.

This creates alignment between the life you want to live and the space that holds it. Your home is more than where you live. It's where you grow. It's where you become.

So before you change anything, ask yourself: What do I need in this season?

Not what looks good. Not what someone else expects. What supports me right now?

The Power Pause: Aligning Your Space with Your Life

Option 1: The 30-Day Reset

As you clear each space, ask:

- What does this space currently communicate?

- What do I want it to communicate instead?

Option 2: Mental + Emotional Declutter

After identifying mental clutter, ask:

- Is this something I need to carry or something I can release?

- What would create more clarity here?

The Shift at Home

Your home is more than a container. It's a mirror. When you care for it with intention, it starts reflecting a different version of you—the one who isn't waiting for a perfect moment to arrive. This is where agency meets your environment. Where inner work becomes visible. Where you remember the life you want starts right here. Next up: taking everything you've learned and stepping fully into your own story.

Chapter 8
Taking Action Toward the Life You Want

Some seasons call for giant leaps, but most change begins quietly. One small, deliberate step can shift the entire direction of your life.

When It's Not Light

Some chapters of life are easy to move through. The air feels lighter, the steps come easier, and hope speaks fluently.

But there are other chapters—the heavy ones—where taking one small step feels like moving a mountain. Where the walls seem closer. Where hope feels like a language you used to speak but can't quite remember anymore.

If that's where you are right now, this chapter is for you. If things feel too big to fix with a few decluttering tips or mindset shifts, I want you to hear this clearly: You are not weak for needing help. You are human.

You Can't DIY Everything

I'm a doer by nature. I like to solve puzzles, build systems, and fix what's broken. But there came a point when sheer willpower wasn't enough. When no amount of lists, lightbulb moments, or environmental shifts could pull me out of the heaviness alone.

> There are some battles we can't DIY our way through.

When I was in the thick of my own crisis—the one I shared with you at the beginning of this book—it took a tribe to get me through. Doctors. Therapists. Coaches. Medication. Movement. Faith. Time. I could not have clawed my way back to life alone. You don't have to either.

Growth was never meant to be a solo project. Neither is becoming. You don't just build a life with your own hands. Just like a literal home, the vision is yours. But the reality? That takes a team.

The Light Moments Count, Too

Not every kind of help looks like a therapy session. Sometimes, it's simply not carrying the weight alone.

In our house, we have a silly tradition I call "The Tidy Ten." Everyone gathers in the same room. I set a timer for ten minutes, and we all clean like we're in a competition for Olympic gold. It's chaotic, hilarious, and it works.

That ten minutes reminds me of something bigger: Shared effort makes heavy things lighter. Like when it's time to move grandma and time to lift the sleeper sofa that she got in 1975 made of solid steel framing with the "good mattress"... aren't you thankful that alllll the cousins show up when it's time to load that bad boy?

> The weight hasn't changed, but shared effort makes heavy things lighter.

Momentum doesn't come from doing everything alone. It comes from reducing resistance. And sometimes, the fastest way forward is to stop trying to carry everything by yourself.

Hiring My First Coach

I can trace a major turning point in my life to one decision: hiring a coach. Ironically, I hired her to help me write a book. (Full circle-moment, right?)

But what really happened was something far deeper. That decision cracked something open in me. It showed me what happens when I allow myself to be supported. Looking back, the spark that set it all in motion wasn't something that felt miraculous. It was more like me making space to allow something new to grow alongside what was still there. Then taking small actions, layered over time, wrapped in a willingness to be helped. What you feed grows.

One day you look around with a smile and say how in the

world did I get here? Then you have a moment of clarity and you know exactly how. You see the flash of all the people who hugged you when you needed it, the laughter with that friend who showed up when you thought all you could do was cry, the doctor who fiiinally listened, the trainer who made you believe you were strong...

The Power of Receiving Help

We love to glorify independence, but real strength often looks like interdependence, knowing when to carry something and when to share the load.

Interdependence isn't codependence. It's shared pulling, the team approach.

There's no shame in saying, "You know what? Let's hire this out." But let's be honest, we often still feel like a boss when we hire and build collaboration. When that professional organizer and painter show up? Please, I'm high steppin' all day!

Then there's the other, less glamorous form of asking for help. The help that comes when we haven't really asked, we've more like accepted it, and maybe with an eye roll. Just so whoever will shut up and not stage an intervention (joking, not joking, if you know, you know). Even in those less glamorous forms of accepting help, it's still a power move. No matter if you ugly cry the whoooole way through.

I want you to hear me on this. It shows strength of character to admit we are on a path that's not helping us—that what we have to carry is larger and heavier than any one person could or should bear the weight of on their own. When we not only are willing to accept a helping hand, but raise our hand and say, "I need backup" that takes power.

That takes self awareness and a maturity that not everyone possesses. But you do.

Asking for help builds the scaffolding around you so you can rise, and do so safely. The version of you you're becoming isn't meant to carry the weight alone.

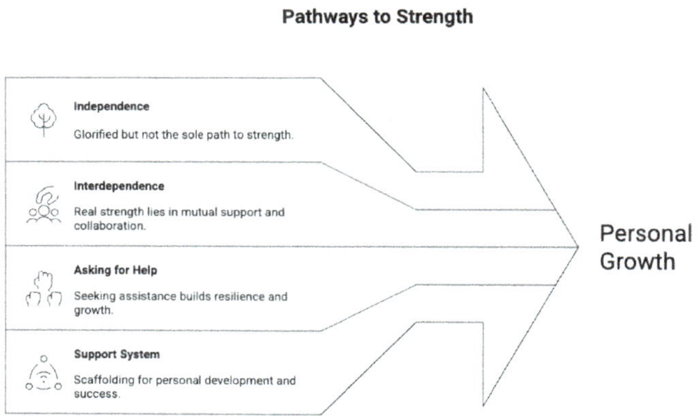

Pathways to Strength

Don't Give Up on You

I know what it feels like to be too tired to hope. To want to tap out of the fight because the hill seems too steep. But please, don't give up on you.
Failure isn't final. It's a data point. A nudge. Feedback. A detour isn't the end of the road, it's a bend you didn't see coming.

You can have a failure, without being a failure. You can be tired, and still not quit.

A Gentle Push Forward

Action creates momentum. Not grand, cinematic action. Just real, small, deliberate steps.

- A list made in the morning.

- A phone call for help.

- A single drawer cleared.

- A walk, a breath or a prayer.

These are the quiet moments that build the loud ones. You may not feel like you're building a new life yet, but you are.

The Power Pause: Taking Aligned Action

Option 1. The One-Year Plan

Set three specific, doable goals you want to move toward in the next year. These can be small quiet goals or big audacious dreams. Break each one down into:

- Quarterly milestones

- Monthly actions

- One small thing you can do this week

Option 2. Habit Builder

Write down one daily habit that supports your growth. Just one. Commit to it for 30 days, not to change everything at once, but to prove to yourself that movement is possible.

Option 3. Ask for Help

Make a list of the areas where you're trying to DIY everything alone. Circle one.

Now, write down one person, resource, or professional who could help you carry that load—and reach out, even if it's just a single message.

The Quiet Kind of Strength

There will be seasons when action looks like a sprint. Others when it looks like standing, leaning, or letting someone else hold the light for you.

No matter the pace, forward is forward. The life you want is built in quiet, relentless steps, not a single leap. Some loud, some soft, but all sacred.

You are not behind. You are becoming. Every small act, from the clothes you donated or the wall you painted, is proof that you haven't given up on yourself. This is how transformation takes root: in progress, not perfection.

Stepping Into What's Next

This journey began with your space, but it was never just about your space. Every stretch and quiet act of courage has been leading you here: to the moment where the story fully belongs to you.

Let's claim that story . . . and live it out loud!

A Life on Purpose

Coming home is about remembering who you are, choosing what stays, and daring to build a life that feels like yours.

We've walked through some tender places together. We've named fears, faced limiting beliefs, rearranged rooms and thoughts, and cleaned out junk drawers and old stories. We've built a bridge between our home and our heart, between the space we live in and the space we carry inside. If you've made it here to this moment, I want you to hear this clearly: You've already begun.

You don't need to wait for perfect timing. Transformation starts with a single honest decision, a small step, a shift in the way we see ourselves.

Now, whether your house has changed or your heart has, you hold the pen. You get to write the next chapter.

Evicting the Doubter

Let's take a deep breath.

Let go of the tension that fear tried to make a permanent tenant.

Now, let's turn to that anxious little voice that loves to whisper its lies. I'm going to call my doubter "Cody."

Let's look Cody square in the eye and hand him his eviction notice. Because effective immediately, you are no longer welcome in our home. Period. No drama. Pack your things and get to steppin'. And don't try me, because I will call the sheriff on your behind.

As I said at the outset, I wrote this as much for me as I did for you. We all need to relax, relate, and release on any given day. Consider this your permission slip to get loud with those inner bullies—the stories that keep you small, the voices that make you doubt what's already true.

What's True

You can do hard things. You have done hard things.

Now, you get to do them on purpose. This isn't about building a perfect house or flawless life but claiming the space you live in—inside and out—and becoming at home in your own story. This is your breadcrumb trail home. Not just to the house you live in, but to yourself.

So let me just say . . . Welcome home.

The Becoming Home Method™

A practical framework for coming home to yourself again and again. By now, you've felt it.

That moment when something clicks. When you realize the discomfort isn't random. When you see the pattern and sense that change is possible.

That moment wasn't accidental. It was the beginning of what I now call The Becoming Home Method,™ a simple, repeatable process you can return to anytime life feels off, noisy, or misaligned. This is a rhythm—a way of noticing, responding, and growing with intention.

You don't need perfect conditions to use it. You don't need a new house, a new job, or a new version of yourself. You just need honesty, curiosity, and a willingness to begin.

Here's the method. All the tea, no gatekeeping.

Step 1: The Pause

Stop the scroll. Interrupt the fog. The Pause is the moment most people skip—and the moment everything changes. It's when you stop ignoring that something feels off. When you interrupt the noise, the busyness, the autopilot. The Pause doesn't have to be dramatic or elaborate.

My first real pause was a 20-minute car ride home from work, sitting in frustration, not distracting myself, not numbing it away. Just noticing.

The Pause is simply this: Something feels off, and I'm willing to stop long enough to notice it. No fixing yet. No judging. Just awareness.

Step 2: The Amplify

Turn up the volume on the feeling you've been avoiding. Once you pause, something usually surfaces. Circle or note all that apply:

Discomfort

Irritation

Sadness

Anger

Grief

Restlessness

Instead of pushing it down, the Becoming Home Method asks you to turn the volume up. This step creates clarity. When we name the feeling, we stop letting it run the house from behind the walls.

Ask yourself:

- What feeling is most uncomfortable right now?

- Where do I feel it in my body?

- When did it start?

- What situation or circumstance can I trace it back to?

Step 3: The Identify

Where is your inner world showing up in your outer one? This is where the mirror comes in. This step is about pattern recognition, not blame. Your home is communicating with you.

Ask yourself:
- Where is my home reflecting this same feeling?

- Is there a space that feels heavy, neglected, chaotic, or unfinished?

- Where does my environment echo what I'm experiencing internally?

This might look like:
- a cluttered desk mirroring mental overwhelm

- a bedroom that doesn't feel restful during a season of burnout

- a kitchen you avoid when nourishment feels like an afterthought

- boxes never unpacked when you haven't fully "moved into" your life

Step 4: The Modify

Shift the inner first. Then change the outer on purpose. Modification always starts internally. Before you touch a drawer, flip the mental switch and tell yourself, "It's time to grow, and I *can* do this." This is where action meets self-trust. When your inner world and outer environment begin to align, momentum follows.

Then, and only then, we modify the environment. Not all at once. Not perfectly but intentionally.

Ask yourself:

- What's one space where a small change would create real impact?

- What would support the version of me I'm becoming, not the one I'm leaving behind?

- What does this space need to feel lighter, calmer, and more aligned?

You might:

- Clear a surface

- Hang the curtains

- Rearrange the room

- Paint the wall

- Let something go that no longer fits

The Becoming Home Method™ Implementation Model

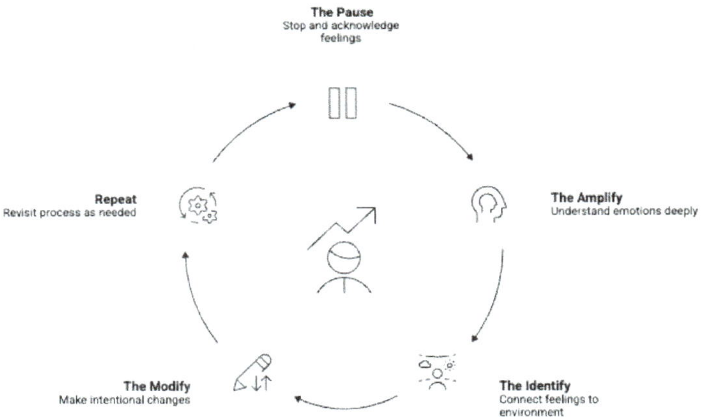

And remember: This isn't something you do once. It's something you return to until your life and your home begin to move in the same direction.

What This Looks Like in Real Life

Different emotions.
Different rooms.
Same method.

When Life Feels Overwhelming

You pause long enough to admit you're not just tired—you're overwhelmed.

You amplify the truth: there's no margin, no space to exhale.

You identify the mirror: Every surface in your home is full.

You modify, starting small, and the relief is immediate.

When Life Feels Stagnant

Nothing is "wrong," but something feels flat.

You amplify the restlessness instead of dismissing it.

You identify the mirror: a workspace that reflects an old version of you.

You modify, clearing what no longer fits and making space for what's next.

The room not only looks better. It feels directional again.

Using the Method Again and Again

You don't complete the Becoming Home Method™. You return to it.

You'll use it:

- When life shifts

- When something feels off

- When you're growing faster than your environment

- When you feel stuck, restless, or ready for more

Each time, you'll notice new layers. Each time, you'll come home a little more fully.

That's the work. That's the gift. It's how you stop waiting for life to change and start participating in it.

The Becoming Home Method™ At a Glance

Before we stretch this back out with real-life examples, here's the framework in its simplest form. This is the repeatable rhythm you can return to anytime something feels off.

Pause: Stop the noise. Interrupt autopilot. Notice that something doesn't feel right without fixing it yet.

Amplify: Turn up the volume on the feeling you've been avoiding. Name it, locate it, then trace it.

Identify: Find where that same feeling is mirrored in your home or environment. Look for the pattern.

Modify: Shift the inner narrative first. Then make a small, intentional change to the outer space to support who you're becoming.

The Becoming Home Method™

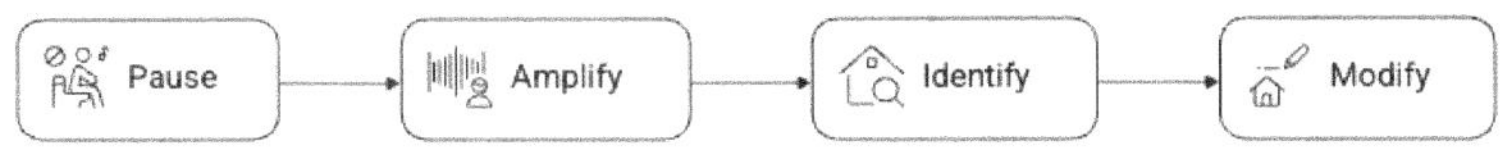

That's it.

Four steps. No drama. No perfection required. Now, let's slow it back down and see how this actually plays out.

The Method in Motion: Two Everyday Scenarios

Scenario One: Overwhelm Without a Name

Pause: You notice you're snapping more easily. You feel mentally foggy and exhausted, even on days that aren't objectively "hard." Instead of scrolling, pushing through, or numbing it out, you stop and admit that something feels off.

Amplify: You ask yourself what feeling is lois the loudestdest? It's overwhelm. Not panic, just constant pressure. You notice it sitting on your chest and shoulders. When you trace it back, you realize there's no margin in your days—no place to land.

Identify: You look around your home and immediately see it. Every surface is full of papers, laundry, and half-finished projects. Your space is carrying the same mental load you are.

Modify: Before touching anything, you flip the internal switch: I don't need to fix my whole life. I just need to support myself better.

You clear one surface. Not the whole room, just one. The relief is subtle but real. Nothing is solved, but alignment has begun.

Scenario Two: Restlessness in a Season That "Should" Feel Fine

Pause: Life looks good on paper. You're functioning. Things are stable. But you feel restless, like you've outgrown something you can't quite name. Instead of ignoring it, you pause and listen.

Amplify: The feeling underneath is readiness, not dissatisfaction. You feel it in your gut. When you trace it back, you realize you're craving expansion, creativity, and momentum.

Identify: You notice your workspace hasn't changed in years. It reflects who you were, not who you're becoming. It's full of old systems, old tools, and old energy.

Modify: You start internally. It's safe to want more. I don't have to justify growth.

Then you make a shift outside. You clear what no longer fits. You update the space to support where you're headed. The room not only looks better and feels directional again.

Why This Works

The Becoming Home Method™ is about listening, aligning, and responding, not pushing, ignoring, or waiting. Your home becomes a partner in your growth, not a silent witness to your burnout. The more you practice this rhythm, the faster you recognize the signals.

You don't wait until things fall apart. You don't wait for permission. You notice, respond, and grow.

That's how you come home—not once, but again and again.

When the Shift Is Bigger Than the Room

Let's talk about the big stuff.

Sometimes you pause . . .

you amplify . . .

you identify . . .

you modify . . .

And the stickiness doesn't go away.

The room looks better.

The space feels lighter.

You did the work.

Yet something still feels off.

That's not failure.

That's information.

This is the moment when the Becoming Home Method™ does something powerful. It tells you the truth, even when the truth is uncomfortable.

The Method Doesn't Always Lead to a Throw Pillow

Sometimes, it leads to a hard conversation, a geographic truth, or a realization you've been avoiding:

It's not the room.

It's the neighborhood.

It's the environment.

It's the chapter.

That realization requires bravery, not decor. This is why real honesty matters most. If you're only willing to accept answers that keep your life exactly the same, the method will stall. If you're willing to listen, really listen, it will guide you where you need to go.

How You'll Know You've Hit a "Big Shift" Moment

The method is signaling something bigger when:

- You've modified your space thoughtfully, and the discomfort persists.

- The same feeling shows up across multiple rooms or areas of life.

- You feel relief temporarily, but the friction returns quickly.

- You sense clarity paired with fear rather than not confusion.

- The answer feels obvious—and terrifying.

- That fear is often a threshold, not a stop sign.

This Is Where Coaching Comes In

Some shifts are meant to be navigated with support because you're standing at a crossroads that affects:

- your finances

- your family

- your identity

- your safety

- your future

These are not decisions to rush or romanticize. Coaching exists to help you move through big transitions with clarity instead of chaos. The Becoming Home Method™ gives you awareness. Coaching helps you translate that awareness into aligned, grounded action.

Your Power Is Knowing What You're Being Asked to Do

You don't have to make the move today. You don't have to blow up your life or have it all figured out. But you do get to know the truth.

Once you know it, you can stop gaslighting yourself with smaller fixes that were never meant to hold a bigger life.

Sometimes, Becoming Home means rearranging a room. Sometimes, it means choosing a new environment entirely.

Both require courage and count as growth, and each begins the same way, with honesty loud enough to hear yourself think.

For the Baddie with a Journal

I f you've made it this far, there's a good chance something in this book resonated with you.

Maybe you saw yourself in a story. Maybe a certain chapter stayed with you. Or maybe you've started looking at your home—and your life—just a little differently.

This section is for when you're ready to go deeper. You can use these prompts:

- after finishing a chapter that stirred something in you

- when your home starts to feel "off" again

- during a life transition or decision-making season

- or anytime you feel the need to reset, reflect, and realign

There's no right or wrong way to do this. Just bring your journal, your honesty, and a willingness to pay attention.

Awareness: What Am I Noticing?

(Chapters 2 & 3: What It Means to Become Home + Your Home Reflects You)

In the earlier chapters, you were introduced to a new way of seeing your home—not just as a place you live, but as a reflection of your life. These questions will help you begin noticing what your environment may be revealing to you.

- What areas of my home feel most aligned right now? Why?

- What areas feel heavy, chaotic, or unfinished?

- Where do I feel most at peace in my home?

- Where do I feel tension, avoidance, or discomfort?

- If my home could speak, what would it say about my current life?

Alignment: Does My Space Reflect My Life Today?

(Chapters 4 & 5: Shattering Limiting Beliefs + Rebuilding the Home Within)

As you began examining your beliefs and rebuilding your internal foundation, you may have noticed that your environment hasn't fully caught up. These prompts will help you explore where your home may still be reflecting a past version of you.

- In what ways has my life changed in the past year?

- Does my home reflect who I am today or who I used to be?

- What in my space no longer fits this season of life?

- What parts of my home support my current priorities?

- Where am I holding onto something that no longer serves me?

Permission: What Am I Ready to Release or Change?

(Chapter 6: When "I Can't" Becomes "I Won't")

By now, you've likely identified areas where change is needed, but awareness alone isn't enough. This is the moment where you decide whether you will stay where you are or step into something new.

- Where have I been telling myself "it's fine" when it's not?

- What changes have I been avoiding and why?

- What am I afraid will happen if I make a change?

- What would I do differently if I fully trusted myself?

- Where do I need to give myself permission to evolve?

Becoming: What Am I Stepping Into?

(Chapters 7 & 8: Your Home is a Platform for Growth + Taking Action Toward the Life You Want)

Your home is not just a reflection of your past; it is a tool for your future. These prompts will help you clarify who you are becoming and how your environment can support that next chapter.

- Who am I becoming in this next season of life?

- What does that version of me value most?

- What kind of environment would support that version of me?

- What needs to be added, removed, or redesigned to support that growth?

- What is one small change I can make this week to move in that direction?

Bringing It All Together

As you've worked through these reflections, you may have started to notice patterns.

Areas that feel clear. Areas that feel heavy. Areas quietly asking for change.

This is where transformation begins. Not by fixing everything at once, but by becoming aware of what your environment is revealing and choosing to respond with intention. Start small. When you're ready, return to the Becoming Home Method and start with Pause. Remember, your home isn't asking you to be perfect. It's asking you to pay attention.

The Becoming Home Quiz Suite

I don't know about you, but I love a good quiz! It takes me back to the days of excitedly curling up with my latest "Seventeen" magazine hoping it will read the depths of my soul and make me feel less awkward and just like everyone else. Even today, somehow I just feel seen by them. So this quiz section is my gift to the angsty teen in all of us who just wants to know we're normal.

Each quiz has the power to stand alone and can gently guides through the method: Pause → Amplify → Identify → Modify

QUIZ 1: Where Are You Stuck Right Now?

(The Pause Quiz)

Answer honestly—not how you wish things felt, but how they do right now.

1. Lately, life feels mostly like…

A. Loud and overwhelming

B. Heavy and exhausting

C. Fine on the outside, off on the inside

D. Stuck or stalled

E. Like something is changing but I can't name it yet

2. When you finally slow down, what shows up first?

A. Mental noise

B. Emotional fatigue

C. Frustration or irritation

D. A sense of "this isn't it anymore"

E. Restlessness or longing

3. Your current season feels…

A. Overfull

B. Under-supported

C. Unfinished

D. Misaligned

E. Transitional

4. When something feels off, you tend to…

A. Stay busy

B. Push through

C. Tidy or organize

D. Daydream about a different life

E. Avoid thinking about it (think daily binge watching)

5. The area that feels heaviest right now is…

A. My mind

B. My energy

C. My space

D. My sense of direction

E. My relationships

6. Deep down, you're craving…

A. Quiet

B. Relief

C. Clarity

D. Change

E. Permission

7. When you look around your home, you most often feel…

A. Overstimulated

B. Drained

C. Annoyed or unsettled

D. Disconnected

E. Like it doesn't quite match where you're headed

8. Your thoughts lately feel...

A. Constant and racing

B. Heavy and slow

C. Reactive or easily triggered

D. Confused or unclear

E. Curious but unsettled

9. When you think about making a change, you feel...

A. Overwhelmed before you begin

B. Too tired to start

C. Like you should fix what's already there first

D. Unsure what direction to take

E. Like something is shifting, but you're not ready yet

10. If someone gave you a completely free day, you would most want to...

A. Sit in silence and decompress

B. Rest without responsibility

C. Reset or clean something

D. Think about your future

E. Just be... without pressure to decide anything

If your answers were spread out, you may be experiencing more than one layer at once. Start with the one that feels easiest and most present.

TALLY SECTION

Count your answers. Circle your highest letter.

A = ___

B = ___

C = ___

D = ___

E = ___

RESULTS

Mostly A → Mental Overload

Your system is overfilled. This is your invitation to pause before adding one more thing.

Mostly B → Emotional Burnout

You've been strong for a long time. This season is asking for care, not endurance.

Mostly C → Environmental Stagnation

Your space may be holding more than it should because you've grown.

Mostly D → Identity Drift

You're not lost. You're between versions. This is a powerful place to be, if you listen.

Mostly E → Transition Tension

Something is shifting under the surface. You don't need answers yet, just honesty.

Don't spiral…the next step isn't fixing. It's listening to what your life is trying to tell you.

QUIZ 2: What Feeling Are You Avoiding?

(The Amplify Quiz)

We don't avoid feelings because we're weak. We avoid them because they're trying to tell us something we may not want to hear.

1. The emotion you least want to feel is…

A. Anger
B. Sadness
C. Fear
D. Disappointment
E. Grief

2. When that emotion shows up, you usually…

A. Minimize it
B. Rationalize it
C. Stay busy
D. Power through
E. Shut down

3. That feeling tends to show up when…

A. I'm alone
B. I'm overwhelmed
C. I feel unseen

D. I'm exhausted

E. I think about the future

4. Where do you feel tension most often?

A. Jaw/neck

B. Chest

C. Stomach

D. Shoulders

E. Low energy overall

5. If that feeling could speak, it would say…

A. "Enough."

B. "Something needs to change."

C. "I'm tired."

D. "This matters."

E. "Pay attention."

6. The thought you push away most is…

A. "I can't keep doing this."

B. "I want more."

C. "I'm resentful."

D. "I'm scared to change."

E. "I don't know who I am anymore."

7. When you feel overwhelmed, your instinct is to…

A. Get irritated or short

B. Withdraw emotionally

C. Overthink everything

D. Push yourself harder

E. Numb out or disconnect

8. The feeling you avoid most often leaves you…

A. On edge or reactive

B. Heavy or low

C. Anxious or unsettled

D. Frustrated with yourself

E. Disconnected or checked out

9. If you slowed down long enough, you suspect you might feel…

A. Angry about what you've tolerated

B. Sad about what you've lost

C. Afraid of what could change

D. Disappointed in where you are

E. Grief for what no longer fits

10. What feels hardest to admit right now?

A. "Something needs to stop."
B. "Something needs to be released."
C. "I don't feel secure."
D. "This isn't working anymore."
E. "I've outgrown this version of my life."

TALLY SECTION

Count your answers. Circle your highest letter.

A = ___
B = ___
C = ___
D = ___
E = ___

RESULTS

Mostly A → Anger → Boundaries

Anger isn't the problem. It's a signal that something has crossed a line. There's likely something you've tolerated for too long, and your system is asking you to respond.

Mostly B → Sadness → Letting Go

Sadness often appears when it's time to release what once mattered. This isn't weakness. It's your capacity to feel what's changing.

Mostly C → Fear → Safety & Support

Fear isn't failure. It's your system trying to protect you. This may be a moment to build support, not avoid movement.

Mostly D → Frustration → Misalignment

You're trying to move forward with outdated conditions Frustration is often a signal that something in your life no longer fits.

Mostly E → Numbness → Overload / Grief

Numbness isn't apathy. It's protection. Your system may be asking for rest, space, or time to process what's too much to feel all at once.

You may see yourself in more than one of these. Start with the one that feels closest to the surface. Take a deep breath...Now that you've named it, let's see where it's showing up.

QUIZ 3: What Is Your Home Reflecting Back To You?

(The Identify Quiz)

Your home isn't judging you. It's talking to you. Use this to tune into what it's saying.

1. The room you avoid most is…

A. Bedroom
B. Kitchen
C. Living room
D. Office
E. Entryway

2. The space that feels most unfinished is…

A. Bedroom
B. Kitchen
C. Living room
D. Office
E. Closet/storage

3. The room you feel calmest in is...

A. Bedroom
B. Kitchen
C. Living room
D. Office
E. None right now

4. Which feels truest right now?

A. I don't feel rested at home
B. I feel depleted or disconnected from nourishment
C. I feel disconnected from my home
D. I feel unclear about my direction
E. My home feels transitional

5. If your home could ask for one thing, it would be...

A. Rest
B. Care
C. Connection
D. Focus
E. Intention

6. When you walk into your home, your first feeling is…

A. Tired

B. Drained

C. Disconnected

D. Mentally cluttered

E. In-between

7. The space that collects the most "stuff" is…

A. Bedroom (laundry, clutter, unfinished rest)

B. Kitchen (dishes, food, surfaces)

C. Living room (general overflow)

D. Office/work area (papers, tasks, ideas)

E. Entryway/closet (things in transition)

8. The space that feels most like "not me anymore" is…

A. Bedroom

B. Kitchen

C. Living room

D. Office

E. The whole house feels in-between

9. If one space in your home felt completely aligned, it would help you feel…

A. Rested
B. Nourished
C. Connected
D. Focused
E. Grounded in what's next

TALLY SECTION

Count your answers. Circle your highest letter.

A = ___
B = ___
C = ___
D = ___
E = ___

RESULTS

Mostly A → Bedroom → Rest & Intimacy

This space reflects how safe you feel slowing down. If this area feels heavy or neglected, it may mirror your relationship with rest, vulnerability, or receiving.

Mostly B → Kitchen → Nourishment & Capacity

This space reflects how you care for yourself. Avoidance here often signals depletion, not laziness. Your life may be asking for support, not more effort.

Mostly C → Living Room → Connection & Belonging

This space mirrors how open you feel to connection. If it feels off, it may reflect disconnection from others, or even from yourself.

Mostly D → Office → Purpose & Clarity

This space reflects your direction and confidence. Clutter here often echoes uncertainty, not lack of ability. You may not just need clarity to get unstuck.

Mostly E → Entryway / Transitional Spaces → Identity & Transition

This space reflects how you're moving between seasons. If things feel in-between, it's transition. Your life may be shifting before your environment has caught up. No space is random. It's all saying something.

QUIZ 4: Is This a Small Shift or a Bigger Brave Move?

(The Modify / Discernment Quiz)

Sometimes clarity comes quietly. Sometimes it asks for courage. Use this to decide which one you need and how to proceed.

1. You've already tried changing your space and…

A. It helped a lot
B. It helped briefly
C. It didn't touch the feeling
D. I haven't tried yet

2. The discomfort feels…

A. Localized
B. Layered
C. Persistent
D. All-encompassing

3. When you imagine staying exactly where you are…

A. I feel okay
B. I feel tired
C. I feel restless
D. I feel heavy

4. When you imagine something bigger changing…

A. Relief
B. Fear
C. Both
D. A sense of knowing

5. The thought you keep circling back to is…

A. "I just need to tweak a few things."
B. "I've outgrown this."
C. "I'm scared to admit what I want."
D. "I already know."

6. If you're honest, the fear is really about…

A. Effort
B. Judgment
C. Uncertainty
D. Disrupting others

7. When you picture your life one year from now, you hope…

A. Things feel more organized and manageable
B. Things feel more stable and supported
C. Things feel different in a meaningful way
D. You're living something you haven't fully admitted yet

8. The tension you feel right now is mostly…

A. In one specific area

B. Showing up in multiple areas

C. Following you everywhere

D. Hard to define, but undeniable

9. What feels most true about your current space?

A. It needs refinement

B. It needs consistency

C. It no longer fits me

D. It represents a version of me I'm ready to leave behind

10. If you removed fear from the equation, you would…

A. Make small changes right where you are

B. Adjust several areas gradually

C. Make a significant shift

D. Choose something you've been avoiding saying out loud

TALLY SECTION

Count your answers. Circle your highest letter.

A = ___

B = ___

C = ___

D = ___

E = ___

RESULTS

Mostly A → Small, Meaningful Shift

A focused change could bring real relief. You don't need to overhaul your life. You need to support it more intentionally. Start small. Clarity will follow.

Mostly B → Layered Change

This is a sequence of decisions and changes You're in a season of building, not jumping. Small, consistent shifts will create stability over time.

Mostly C → Bigger Transition

The signal is clear. The timing is yours. Something in your life no longer fits. You don't need to rush, but you do need to acknowledge it.

Mostly D → You Already Know

Courage isn't about speed, it's about truth This isn't confusion, it's resistance to what you already see. Your next step is honoring it.

Becoming Home Quick Reset

When life feels off and you feel like texting your bestie "911!" Start here.

1. Find Your Starting Point

What feels most true right now? Don't overthink it. Pick one.

- Everything feels loud or overwhelming → Pause

- I can't name what I'm feeling → Amplify

- My home feels off or disconnected → Identify

- I'm stuck between staying or changing → Modify

2. Tell the Truth

Not the polished version. The real one. Awareness first. Always.

- What feels off?

- What am I avoiding?

- Where is this showing up in my space?

3. Make One Small Shift

Not everything. Just one action. Small shifts create momentum.

- Clear one surface

- Sit with one feeling

- Make one decision

- Ask for one piece of help

4. Use the Becoming Home Method™

- Pause → Notice it

- Amplify → Feel it

- Identify → See where it's showing up

- Modify → Shift one thing

- Repeat → Come back when needed

5. Check Your Season

What do I need right now? Let your home match your season.

- Survival → simplify, stabilize

- Stability → organize, support

- Growth → design, expand

Remember…You're not stuck. Your life is responding. So change the input:

- your environment

- your patterns

- your next small decision

Final Thought

You don't need a new life to begin again. Just: one space, one truth, one shift. Start there.

Guided Index

A chapter-by-chapter reference for reflection, application, and return.

INTRODUCTION — The Decision to Live

Core Themes

- Choosing life in the middle of pain

- Awareness before transformation

- The moment everything can shift

Key Concepts

- The decision to live vs. exist

- Crisis as a catalyst

- Hope as a turning point

Use This Section When

- You feel overwhelmed or at rock bottom

- You need a reminder that your story isn't over

CHAPTER 1 — Life Happens, But You Decide

Core Themes

- Personal responsibility and authorship

- Breaking cycles

- Environment as a lever for change

Key Concepts

- Life doesn't just happen to you.

- Your home as a mirror + tool

- Outer change influencing inner change

Notable Ideas

- "Your home is diagnostic and therapeutic."

Use This Section When

- You feel stuck in your circumstances

- You need to reclaim agency

CHAPTER 2 — What It Means to Become Home

Core Themes

- Home as an energetic and sensory experience

- Environment + identity feedback loop

Key Concepts

- Home = mirror + feedback system

- Environment affects mood, energy, behavior

- Sensory inputs (light, sound, layout)

- Einstein reference (matter = energy interaction)

- Sensory environment impact

Use This Section When

- You feel "off" but can't explain why

- You want to understand why your space affects you

CHAPTER 3 — Your Home Reflects You

Core Themes

- Awareness through environment

- The mirror effect

- Small shifts → big impact

Key Concepts

- Inner vs. outer world

- Pattern recognition

- Momentum through action

Exercises

- Power Pause: Room walkthrough

- Photo rating exercise

Use This Section When

- You want a starting point

- You need clarity without overthinking

CHAPTER 4 — Shattering Limiting Beliefs

Core Themes

- Invisible mental blockers

- Fear disguised as logic

- Stretch before transformation

Key Concepts

- Limiting beliefs as "safety systems"

- Back-door transformation (environment first)

- The "stretch moment"

Exercises

- Limiting belief journal

- Self-talk audit

Use This Section When

- You feel resistance to change

- You keep circling the same patterns

CHAPTER 5 — Rebuilding the Home Within

Core Themes

- Identity rebuilding

- Patterns + repetition

- Life as a system

Key Concepts

- Action → Pattern → Life result

- Momentum (Newton's Law)

- Neuroplasticity (repetition rewires)

- Life as a system output

- It's not failure, it's feedback.

Exercises

- System awareness reflection

Use This Section When

- You've made a change but feel wobbly

- You want structure after courage

CHAPTER 6 — When "I Can't" Becomes "I Won't"

Core Themes

- Language → belief → behavior → results

- Personal agency

- Cognitive reframing

Key Concepts

- "I can't" = perceived limitation

- "I won't" = ownership + choice

- Perspective (lens) shapes reality

- Brain filters for confirmation

- Thought repetition builds outcomes

Exercises

- "I can't → I won't" reframing

- Mindset tracking

Use This Section When

- You feel powerless

- You're avoiding a decision

CHAPTER 7 — Your Home Is a Platform for Growth

Core Themes

- Environment as a growth tool

- Layered transformation

- Alignment with life seasons

Key Concepts

- Maslow's Hierarchy applied to home

- Environment affects nervous system

- Your home reinforces identity

- The Home Transformation Pyramid™

- Cleaning & Decluttering (foundation)

- Organizing (structure)

- Design (growth)

- The Pyramid of Priority

- Life seasons → shifting needs

Exercises

- 30-Day Reset

- Mental + emotional declutter

Use This Section When

- You're ready for action

- You want to improve your space strategically

CHAPTER 8 — Taking Action Toward the Life You Want

Core Themes

- Action in hard seasons

- Interdependence (not doing life alone)

- Momentum through small steps

Key Concepts

- You can't DIY everything

- Shared effort reduces resistance

- Support = strength

Notable Ideas

- Shared effort makes heavy things lighter.

- Growth requires support systems

Exercises

- Ask for help exercise

- Load-sharing reflection

Use This Section When

- Life feels too heavy

- You're trying to do everything alone

CONCLUSION — A Life on Purpose

Core Themes

- Ownership of your story

- Integration of inner + outer life

- Becoming as a lifelong process

Key Concepts

- Evicting limiting voices ("Cody")

- Choosing intentionally

- Living on purpose

Use This Section When

- You need encouragement

- You're stepping into a new chapter

APPENDIX: The Becoming Home Method

Steps

Pause + Amplify + Identify + Modify + Repeat

Use When

- Something feels off

- You need a repeatable reset process

Reflection Prompts Section Organized By Chapter Themes

- Awareness (Ch. 2–3)

- Alignment (Ch. 4–5)

- Permission (Ch. 6)

- Becoming (Ch. 7–8)

Use When

- You want deeper clarity

- You're journaling or making decisions

Quiz Suite Index

Quiz 1 — Pause

Where Are You Stuck Right Now?
   Identifies your current state (mental, emotional, environmental)

Quiz 2 — Amplify

What Feeling Are You Avoiding?
   Identifies emotional signal

Quiz 3 — Identify

What Is Your Home Reflecting?
Connects emotion → environment

Quiz 4 — Modify

Small Shift or Big Move?
Discernment + decision-making

Use When

You want quick clarity or you feel stuck but can't name why.

A Gentle Next Step

This book was never meant to give you all the answers. It was meant to help you hear your own. If what you're hearing now points toward a bigger shift, one that deserves care, strategy, and real honesty, coaching is one way to support that process. You're still in the driver's seat. Support steadies your power.

When and if you decide you'd like guidance as you navigate what comes next, that door is open. Learn more about working with Becoming Home author, Kendra Jarrell at consultwithkendra.com/.

Acknowledgements

There are very few things in life created alone, and this isn't one of them. This book may have my name on it, but it was shaped over years of experiences, conversations, and quiet realizations that didn't happen in isolation. While this journey began in a very personal place, it didn't stay there. It expanded.

Through the women I've worked with, learned from, and observed over the years, women who built beautiful lives and still found themselves navigating moments of quiet overwhelm, I saw you. Those moments mattered. They helped give language to what this book would eventually become.

To the people who have welcomed me into their homes as a guide for what's next: Thank you for viewing me as a safe space at a time when things can feel scary and overwhelming. I've seen the transformations you've made to your spaces and how they made room for who you were becoming.

To the people who supported this work in tangible ways—with your time, your insight, your encouragement—it all played a role in bringing this to life.

And to the spaces, seasons, and experiences that have shaped me along the way…Thank you. This book is about more than home as a place. It's about the ongoing process of becoming. And that process is never created alone.

Kendra Jarrell

Kendra Jarrell is the author of *Becoming Home: Self-Discovery Through the Power of Space*, a book that reframes how women navigate life transitions by learning how to read what's actually happening beneath the surface. With a background in real estate, design, and advisory work, she has spent years guiding clients through relocation, custom home-building, and major life shifts. Along the way, she noticed a pattern that most women weren't lacking options, they were carrying too much, and making decisions from that weight. Kendra's work uses space, season, and lifestyle design as tools to understand what's really going on, so women can move forward with clarity, steadiness, and far less second-guessing. Connect with her at consultwithkendra.com/.